To

Glenn & Ian

From

Don 1996

D0966204

JOHN HADAMUSCIN'S

Sheer
Indulgences

Also by John Hadamuscin

JOHN HADAMUSCIN'S
DOWN HOME
*A Year of Cooking, Entertaining,
and Living Easy*

JOHN HADAMUSCIN'S
SIMPLE PLEASURES
*101 Thoughts and Recipes for
Savoring the Little Things in Life*

JOHN HADAMUSCIN'S
FROM MY HOUSE TO YOURS
*Gifts, Recipes, and Remembrances
from the Hearth and Home*

JOHN HADAMUSCIN'S
ENCHANTED EVENINGS
Dinners, Suppers, Picnics, and Parties

SPECIAL OCCASIONS
Holiday Entertaining All Year Round

THE HOLIDAYS
*Elegant Entertaining from
Thanksgiving to Twelfth Night*

JOHN HADAMUSCIN'S
Sheer
Indulgences

*Thoughts and Recipes for
Savoring the Extravagances of Life*

Photographs by Randy O'Rourke

HARMONY BOOKS / NEW YORK

Book design by Ken Sansone
Thanks to Cathy, Ed, Michael, and Steven Stuzynski

Copyright ©1994 by John Hadamuscin
Photographs copyright © 1994 by Randy O'Rourke
Photograph on page 47 copyright © 1994 by J. Barry O'Rourke

Published by Harmony Books, a division of Crown Publishers, Inc.
201 East 50th Street, New York, New York 10022.
Member of the Crown Publishing Group.
Random House, Inc. New York, Toronto, London, Sydney, Auckland

HARMONY and colophon are trademarks of Crown Publishers, Inc.
Manufactured in China

Library of Congress Cataloging-in-Publication Data

Hadamuscin, John.
John Hadamuscin's sheer indulgences:
thoughts and recipes for savoring the extravagances of life/
photographs by Randy O'Rourke.
p.cm.
Includes index.
1.Cookery. I. Title. II. Title: Sheer indulgences.
TX714.H34   1994
641.5—dc20   94-8649
CIP

ISBN 0-517-59920-1
10 9 8 7 6 5 4 3 2 1
First Edition

INTRODUCTION

$\mathcal{W}$hen you experience that moment, it's just glorious!"
My friend Janet was talking about the moment when you give
in and indulge yourself. For me, that moment may come in a
restaurant when, after having grilled fish, steamed vegetables,
and a salad for dinner, I go right ahead and order a gooey dessert,
even after telling myself I wouldn't give in. Or when I just can't
pass that flower stand without buying those calla lilies. Or the
moment may come as it did when I was shopping for a new car
and, rather than examining the practical 4 x 4 that I'd come in
to look at, I test-drove a zippy yellow convertible instead.

In that moment of giving way to an immediate yearning,
some of us might think of faraway places and others might
dream of fancy cars, riches, and Champagne. I think of those
things too, but I also think of having tea, with scones slathered
with strawberry preserves and clotted cream, or soaking in a
scented bath after a long day. Yet another example is when
I'm dieting, which is about all the time; I allow myself one
treat a week, a "little" indulgence like a fudgy Brownie
Pudding "All the Way."

"Sheer indulgence" is giving in to something out of the ordinary and making an
extraordinary gift to oneself. It's that   little act of
selfishness whether we're happy   or whether we need
a little cheering up. It's a   step beyond what we allow
ourselves on a day-to-day   basis. And every once in a while,
there's nothing wrong   with that! So be good to yourself,
give in—eat some-   thing gooey, or buy yourself flowers—
and then savor   the moment.

John

Hazelnut–Fudge Bread Puddings

MAKES 6 INDIVIDUAL PUDDINGS

Custardy, chocolaty bread pudding seems extra-special when baked in individual dishes—maybe it's because you get to eat the whole thing all by yourself!

6 ounces (6 squares) semisweet chocolate, coarsely chopped
2 tablespoons unsalted butter
1 ¼ cups milk
¾ cup sugar
¼ teaspoon salt
1 tablespoon rum
2 large eggs, lightly beaten
1 teaspoon vanilla extract
1 ½ cups coarse, soft crumbs from firm, good-quality day-old white bread
½ cup chopped hazelnuts, lightly toasted
1 cup (½ pint) heavy cream, whipped
Shavings of semisweet chocolate

1. Preheat the oven to 350°F. Lightly grease six 6-ounce ramekins or other shallow 6-ounce baking dishes and place them in a shallow baking pan.

2. Combine the chocolate and butter in the top of a double boiler over simmering water and stir until melted and smooth, about 5 minutes.

3. Stir in the milk, sugar, salt, and rum and stir again until smooth. Remove the double boiler from the heat and stir in the eggs and vanilla. Add the bread crumbs and the nuts, then stir again until blended in.

4. Divide the batter among the prepared ramekins. Pour hot tap water into the outer baking pan to come halfway up the outsides of the ramekins. Place the pan in the oven and bake until the puddings are set, 40 to 45 minutes.

5. Serve the puddings warm or chilled, with a generous dollop of whipped cream and a sprinkling of chocolate shavings.

Buying yourself flowers

Lobster Medallions in Port and Peppercorn Sauce over Spinach Fettuccine

SERVES 4

When I was growing up in Ohio, lobster was just not in our vocabulary. Nowadays this succulent seafood is much more readily available everywhere, but it still always seems like a special treat to me, no matter whether I have it in a restaurant or at home.

4 lobster tails
4 tablespoons all-purpose flour, approximately
4 tablespoons (½ stick) unsalted butter
2 large garlic cloves, crushed
2 tablespoons tawny Port
1 cup dry white wine
1 cup water
½ teaspoon dry mustard
1 tablespoon drained green peppercorns (see Note)
¼ cup chopped parsley
½ cup heavy cream
1 pound spinach fettuccine

1. Remove the lobster meat from the shell in one piece, then slice the meat crosswise into ½-inch-thick medallions. Dredge the lobster medallions in the flour, lightly coating them on all sides.

2. Place a medium, heavy skillet over medium heat and add 2 tablespoons of the butter and the garlic. When the butter begins to sizzle and color slightly, add the lobster medallions and lightly brown them on both sides. Remove the medallions from the pan and keep warm.

3. Add the Port, white wine, water, mustard, peppercorns, and parsley to the skillet. Raise the heat to medium-high, bring to a boil, and continue boiling until the mixture is reduced by half, 5 to 7 minutes. Remove the garlic cloves and discard. Add the cream, bring the sauce to a simmer, and reduce the heat to low. Cook, stirring frequently to prevent sticking, until the sauce thickens slightly, 5 to 7 minutes.

4. Meanwhile, cook the pasta in a large pan of boiling salted water until al dente (timing will depend on the pasta used; check the package for directions). Drain the pasta, return to the pan, and toss with the remaining butter.

5. Return the lobster medallions to the skillet and cook until heated through. Divide the pasta among 4 plates, arrange the medallions over the pasta, and spoon the sauce over all.

NOTE: Green peppercorns are sold packed in brine in small bottles or jars in large grocery stores or fancy food shops.

Lemon Charlotte with Raspberries

SERVES 8 TO 10

Every so often it's fun to have a big, show-stopping, classic dessert. Plan a dinner that's not too heavy or rich, then wait an hour or so after finishing dinner to serve this spectacle.

The traditional French charlotte is usually made with ladyfingers or strips of genoise (sponge cake), but I think pound cake works just fine.

1 tablespoon (1 envelope)
    unflavored gelatin
¾ cup whole milk
4 large eggs, separated
Juice and grated rind
    of 2 lemons
¾ cup sugar
¼ teaspoon salt
½ teaspoon vanilla extract
2 cups (1 pint) heavy cream
1 pound cake, approximately
    9 x 5 x 4 inches, cut into
    ½ x 1 x 3-inch strips
½ pint raspberries
Mint leaves, for garnish

1. In the top of a double boiler over simmering water, combine the gelatin and milk and stir until the gelatin is softened. In a small bowl, lightly beat the egg yolks with the lemon juice and rind, ½ cup sugar, and salt, then gradually stir this mixture into the double boiler. Cook, stirring constantly, until the mixture is thickened and smooth, about 5 minutes. Remove from the heat and stir in the vanilla. Allow the custard mixture to cool.

2. In a clean bowl, beat the egg whites until stiff peaks form. In a separate bowl, beat 1 cup of the cream until soft peaks form. Gradually fold the egg whites and cream into the custard mixture.

3. Using vegetable oil, lightly oil the inside of a deep 2-quart bowl. Line the bowl with pound cake strips. Spoon the custard mixture into the bowl, smooth the top, and cover the bowl with plastic wrap. Chill at least 4 hours or overnight.

4. In the bowl of a food processor fitted with the steel chopping blade, combine half the raspberries with the remaining ¼ cup sugar. Process until the raspberries are pureed, transfer to a small bowl, cover, and chill until serving time. No more than 2 hours before serving time, whip the remaining 1 cup cream until soft peaks form, then chill until serving time.

5. Just before serving, dip the charlotte bowl in a pan of warm water to loosen the charlotte. Unmold the charlotte onto a serving plate. Drizzle the raspberry puree over the charlotte, then spoon the whipped cream over the top. Scatter the raspberries over and around the charlotte and garnish with mint leaves. Cut into thin wedges to serve.

*R*aspberries *out of season*

Eating an entire pint of very good ice cream all by yourself

Salmon Steaks Puttanesca

SERVES 6

Salmon is always a treat, and this unusual preparation is especially rich, moist, and highly flavored. I serve this with sautéed broccoli rabe, but serving it with pasta alongside would make it all the more decadent.

6 ounces button mushrooms, thinly sliced
½ cup dry red wine
2 cups (1 15½-ounce can) canned plum tomatoes in puree
2 large garlic cloves, chopped

½ teaspoon salt
½ teaspoon dried thyme leaves
⅛ teaspoon crushed red pepper flakes, or more to taste
4 bay leaves
1 tablespoon drained capers
6 oil-cured black olives, pitted and coarsely chopped
2 slices lean thinly sliced bacon, chopped
6 salmon steaks, about ½ pound each
1 medium onion, thinly sliced and separated into rings

1. In a small bowl, combine the mushrooms and wine and let stand. Preheat the oven to 400°F.

2. Place the tomatoes in a separate bowl, crushing them into chunks with your hands. Add the garlic, salt, thyme, pepper flakes, bay leaves, capers, and olives and stir well.

3. Place the bacon in a shallow baking dish just large enough to hold the salmon steaks in one layer. Place the dish in the oven until the bacon begins to brown and render its fat, about 10 minutes. Remove the pan from the oven and, using a slotted spoon, transfer the bacon to the tomato mixture and mix well. Remove all but a thin film of the bacon fat from the baking dish.

4. Place the salmon steaks in the baking dish, then scatter the mushroom mixture over them, followed by the onions. Spoon the tomato mixture over all. Bake until the salmon is firm and flakes with a fork, 20 to 25 minutes. Remove the bay leaves.

5. To serve, place 1 steak on each plate. Spoon sauce from the baking dish over each serving.

*S*leeping until two
in the afternoon

*R*eading a trashy
novel all day

*B*elgian Fries

SERVES 4 TO 6

In Brussels, "French" fries (and I'm not talking about the limp and pale imitations sold in fast-food places worldwide) are the semiofficial street food. The Belgian *frites* are crisp on the outside and tender on the inside, beautifully browned, and fragrant, and they're served in big paper cones with a big dab of real mayonnaise for dipping. I like these fries sprinkled with a little salt and a few dashes of malt vinegar.

Vegetable oil or shortening,
*   for frying*
6 large Idaho potatoes
Salt

1. In an electric deep fryer or a

large kettle fitted with a candy or frying thermometer, heat the vegetable oil to a temperature of 370°F. Have ready a frying basket or large strainer.

2. While the oil is heating, cut the potatoes into sticks about ¼ inch thick. Place them in a bowl with water to cover.

3. A large handful at a time, drain the potatoes, dry them well with paper towels, and drop them into the basket. Lower the basket into the hot fat and cook the potatoes until tender but not browned, about 3 minutes.

4. Lift the basket, allowing excess fat to drain off, and spill the potatoes onto absorbent paper to drain and cool. (The potatoes can be prepared in advance, wrapped well, and refrigerated; return to room temperature before proceeding.) Remove the oil from the heat.

5. Reheat the oil to 380°F. In small batches, place the potatoes in the basket, dip the basket into the hot fat, and cook until the potatoes are a deep golden brown, about 5 minutes. Remove the basket from the fat and spill the potatoes out onto a large shallow pan lined with absorbent paper and sprinkle lightly with salt. Serve immediately. (Finished potatoes can be kept warm in a slow oven while frying the remaining ones.)

Chocolate-Filled Almond Cream Puffs

MAKES ABOUT 2 DOZEN

Cream puffs are light, flaky, and delicious, whether they're filled with chocolate mousse or with strawberry ice cream. You always think you can eat more than one, and you usually do.

CREAM PUFFS

½ cup (1 stick) unsalted, softened butter, cut into chunks
1 cup hot tap water
1 cup sifted all-purpose flour
4 large eggs, at room temperature
½ cup sliced almonds

FILLING

1 cup heavy cream
⅓ cup unsweetened cocoa
⅓ cup confectioners' sugar
½ teaspoon vanilla extract
½ teaspoon almond extract
Pinch of salt

Confectioners' sugar, for dusting

1. Preheat the oven to 400°F. Grease a baking sheet well.

2. In a heavy saucepan, combine the butter and water and place over medium heat. Cook until the butter melts and stir well. Lower the heat and gradually blend in the flour. Continue stirring until the mixture forms a

ball, about 1 minute. Remove the pan from the heat and, using a whisk or hand mixer, beat in the eggs one at a time, beating well after each addition.

3. Drop the dough by heaping tablespoonfuls onto the baking sheet about 2 inches apart. Sprinkle the almonds over the dough. Bake for 15 minutes, lower the heat to 350°F., and continue baking until the puffs

are doubled in size and golden brown, about 20 minutes longer. Remove to a wire rack to cool completely before filling.

4. To make the filling, combine all the ingredients in a bowl no more than 2 hours before serving and beat until stiff peaks form. Chill until serving time.

5. To assemble, split the cream puffs horizontally in half. Place the filling in a pastry bag fitted with a large star tip and pipe it into the bottom halves of the cream puffs. Place the top halves over, dust with confectioners' sugar, and serve immediately.

A bed of roses

Peppery Country Ham Pâté

SERVES 10 TO 12
AS AN HORS D'OEUVRE

This rich-tasting pâté goes nicely with beer or cocktails. Serve it with little biscuits or thin toasted slices of baguette.

4 bay leaves
1 thin lemon slice
1 roasted red bell pepper, peeled, seeded, and chopped
1 pound ground cooked country ham
1 pound ground lean pork
2 cups fine, dry bread crumbs
2 large eggs, lightly beaten
3 tablespoons tomato paste
³/₄ cup unsweetened applesauce

1 tablespoon brandy
1 medium onion, chopped
¹/₂ cup chopped parsley
1 teaspoon dry mustard
¹/₄ teaspoon ground cayenne
¹/₄ teaspoon finely ground black pepper
¹/₃ cup apple jelly

1. Preheat the oven to 325°F. Lightly grease a 6-cup loaf pan or ring mold. Arrange the bay leaves and lemon slice in a pattern in the bottom of the pan.

2. In a mixing bowl, combine the chopped roasted pepper, the meats, bread crumbs, eggs, 2 tablespoons of the tomato paste, the applesauce, brandy, onion, parsley, and spices and mix well with your hands. Pack this mixture into the prepared pan and cover the pan tightly with lightly greased aluminum foil.

3. Place the pan into a larger shallow pan or baking dish and pour hot tap water into the larger pan to come halfway up the sides of the inner pan. Bake until firm, about 1½ hours. Remove the pans from the oven, removing the inner pan from the outer one. Pour the water off from the outer pan, then invert the pâté into the larger pan.

4. In a small saucepan over medium heat, combine the apple jelly and the remaining tomato paste and stir until the jelly is melted and the mixture is smooth. Brush this mixture liberally over the pâté, place the pan in the oven, and bake until the pâté is glazed and browned, 20 to 30 minutes.

5. Remove the pan to a wire rack to cool, then loosely cover the pan with foil and chill the pâté overnight to allow the flavor to develop before serving. To unmold, dip the pan in a basin of hot water, run a blunt knife around the edge of the pâté, and invert onto a small cutting board. Cut the pâté into thin slices to serve.

Dinner at the best restaurant in town

A baby grand piano

Jumbo chocolate chip cookies

THE BEST CHOCOLATE CHIPS

I've always said that the best chocolate chip cookie recipe is the one right there on the back of the chocolate chip package, so you won't get a recipe from me. The only hint I offer is to use all brown sugar instead of a mixture of white and brown, and to drop the dough by tablespoonfuls onto the baking sheet for extra-sized cookies.

P.S. It's perfectly all right to eat the cookies right off the rack while they're still warm.

Cherries Jubilee

SERVES 4

Though this classic "fancy" dessert has been replaced by trendier upstarts on most restaurant menus, it hasn't yet gone down in flames. And it's still a spectacular way to end a meal.

2 tablespoons sugar
2 teaspoons cornstarch
Juice and grated rind of $1/2$ orange
1 cup pitted sweet cherries
   (frozen cherries, thawed,
   can be substituted)
$1/3$ cup water
1 pint best-quality vanilla ice
   cream
$1/4$ cup brandy

1. In a small nonreactive skillet or a chafing dish, combine the sugar, cornstarch, and orange juice and rind and place over medium-high heat. Bring to a simmer, stirring constantly. Reduce the heat to low, add the cherries and water, and simmer, stirring occasionally to prevent sticking. (This recipe can be prepared ahead up to this point, trans- ferred to a small bowl, and refrigerated; reheat in the skillet before serving.)

2. Just before serving, scoop the ice cream into 4 stemmed heavy glasses. Add the brandy to the warm cherry mixture in the skillet and bring to just below the simmering point. Remove the pan from the heat and, using caution, ignite the sauce with a long match. When the flames die out, spoon the sauce over the ice cream and serve immediately.

$\mathcal{M}$ile-High Lime Chiffon Pie

MAKES ONE 9-INCH PIE

Here in the northeast, almost every diner has a refrigerated glass-doored case for showing off the "baked on the premises" desserts, from multilayered cakes to mile-high pies. And it works. But unfortunately, the taste of these spectacular sweets almost never lives up to the appearance, so I decided to make one of my own.

GINGERSNAP CRUST
1½ cups fine gingersnap crumbs
¼ cup sugar
6 tablespoons (¾ stick) unsalted
  butter, melted

FILLING
1 tablespoon (1 envelope)
  unflavored gelatin
¼ cup water
1 cup sugar
¼ teaspoon salt
Juice and grated rind of 3
  key limes or 2 regular limes
6 large eggs, separated
1 teaspoon vanilla extract

1. Preheat the oven to 350°F.

2. To make the crust, combine the crumbs and sugar in a small bowl and mix well. Add the melted butter and stir well to moisten all the crumbs. Press the mixture evenly into the bottom and sides of a 9-inch pie pan. Place the pan in the oven and

bake for 8 minutes, then remove the pan to a wire rack to cool.

3. In the top of a double boiler not yet over heat, combine the gelatin and cold water and whisk to dissolve the gelatin. Add ½ cup of the sugar, the salt, lime juice, and egg yolks and whisk until blended.

4. Place the pan over simmering water and cook, whisking constantly, until the mixture reaches the consistency of thick cream, about 7 minutes. Stir in the lime rind and the vanilla and remove from the heat. Transfer the mixture to a medium bowl and chill about 10 minutes to thicken it a bit more.

5. In a spotlessly clean bowl, beat the egg whites until soft peaks form, then gradually beat in the remaining ½ cup sugar, continuing to beat until stiff peaks form. Gradually fold the egg white mixture into the egg yolk mixture. Then spoon the mixture into the cooled pie shell, letting the filling stand in mounds.

6. Chill the pie thoroughly, at least 4 hours, before serving.

VARIATIONS: Stir a drop or two of green food coloring into the egg yolk mixture when it's finished cooking. Add 1 tablespoon rum to the filling at the end of step 3.

A pair of silk pajamas

Flying on the Concorde

Chicken-Fried Steaks with Cream Gravy

SERVES 2 TO 4

This is the classic country-style dish that's probably the richest, most indulgent, and sinful food of all. It starts with beef steaks, which are dipped in egg and breaded, then fried, then served with mashed potatoes on the side and a rich creamy gravy (the gravy's traditionally made with heavy cream, but whole milk is plenty rich enough for me, thanks) slathered all over everything. In a word, dee-licious!

I'll admit that I make this only once in a blue moon (and when I do I always serve it with green beans or asparagus so there's a green vegetable on the plate)—and then I promise myself I'll be good for days after.

2 large eggs, lightly beaten
1 1/2 cups milk
1 cup all-purpose flour
1/2 teaspoon paprika
1/2 teaspoon salt
1 teaspoon coarsely ground
*   black pepper*
1 1/2 pounds beef round steaks,
*   pounded thin*
Lard, for frying (vegetable
*   shortening can be substituted,*
*   if you must)*

1. Combine the eggs and 2 tablespoons of the milk in a shallow bowl and beat with a fork until blended. In a separate shallow bowl, stir the flour, paprika, salt, and pepper together until well blended. One at a time, dip the steaks in the eggs, then dredge them in the seasoned flour; repeat. Place the steaks on a platter and let stand 5 minutes. (Save excess flour for making the gravy.)

2. Place a heavy skillet over medium heat, and melt enough lard to reach a depth of about ½ inch. Heat the lard until it is hot but not smoking, 1 or 2 minutes. Place the steaks in the fat and cook until a deep golden brown on both sides, about 6 minutes on the first side and about 4 minutes on the second. Transfer the steaks to absorbent paper to drain excess fat and keep warm.

3. To make the gravy, pour off all but about 2 tablespoons fat. Add 2 tablespoons of the reserved flour, stirring until well blended and scraping up any browned bits from the bottom of the skillet. Slowly stir in the remaining milk and continue cooking, stirring constantly, until the gravy is thickened and the flour is cooked through, 3 to 5 minutes. Season to taste with salt and plenty of black pepper.

4. Serve the steaks with mashed potatoes on the side, all smothered in the gravy.

½ cup maple syrup
*½ cup (1 stick) unsalted butter,
    melted*
*½ cup firmly packed dark brown
    sugar*
2 teaspoons ground cinnamon
⅔ cup chopped walnuts
 ½ cup dried currants

1. In a small mixing bowl, combine the yeast and warm water and stir to dissolve the yeast. In the bowl of an electric mixer, combine the milk and the melted butter, then beat in the eggs, granulated sugar, and salt. Beat in the yeast mixture.

2. A cup at a time, beat in 5 cups of the flour, then turn the dough out onto a floured work surface and knead in another ½ cup flour at a time to make a soft, non-sticky dough. Knead until smooth and elastic.

3. Shape the dough into a ball, place in a lightly oiled bowl, and cover the bowl with a cloth. Allow the dough to double in bulk, about 1 hour.

4. To make the glaze, combine

$\mathcal{M}$*aple-Walnut*
Sticky Buns

MAKES ABOUT 2 DOZEN

Gooey and nutty with a maple–caramel topping, these are one sinful way to start the day. This recipe makes quite a few, but I'm sure that won't be a problem.

2 envelopes active dry yeast
½ cup warm water
2 cups hot milk
*½ cup (1 stick) unsalted butter,
    melted*
2 large eggs, at room temperature
½ cup granulated sugar
1 teaspoon salt
6½ to 7 cups all-purpose flour

the maple syrup, melted butter, brown sugar, and cinnamon and stir until smooth. Spoon about 2 teaspoons of the mixture into each cup of two 1-dozen non-stick muffin pans, then divide the nuts among the muffin cups.

5. Divide the dough in two and, on the floured work surface, roll each portion out into a rectangle about 15 inches x 8 inches. Brush the surface of each rectangle with about half the remaining glaze and sprinkle the currants over the glaze. Roll up the rectangles,

jelly roll fashion, and cut each into twelve 1¼-inch slices.

6. Place 1 dough slice, cut-side down, into each muffin cup. Cover the pans with cloths and let the dough rise again, about 30 minutes.

7. Preheat the oven to 350°F. Bake the buns until nicely browned, about 25 minutes. Invert the pans onto a wire rack (set over wax paper or aluminum foil to catch drips) to remove the rolls from the pans. Serve warm.

A few days at a cottage by the sea

$\mathcal{P}$ecan-Deviled Shrimp with Red Pepper–Horseradish Mayonnaise

SERVES 4 TO 6

Years ago when dining out, "luxurious" shrimp cocktail was something one ordered only on special occasions. Nowadays, shrimp is less rare and not quite as expensive, but it still has a connotation of luxury. Here's a luxuriously flavored alternative to the old classic.

$^1/_3$ cup sour cream
1 large egg, lightly beaten
$^1/_3$ cup Dijon mustard
$^1/_4$ teaspoon salt
$^1/_4$ teaspoon hot pepper sauce, or more to taste
4 scallions, white and green parts, finely chopped
1 $^1/_2$ cups ground pecans
1 $^1/_2$ pounds large shrimp, peeled and deveined, tails left on
Red Pepper-Horseradish Mayonnaise (recipe follows)

1. Preheat the oven to 400°F. Lightly grease a large baking sheet.

2. In a shallow bowl, combine the sour cream, egg, mustard, salt, hot pepper sauce, and scallions and mix well. Place the pecans in another shallow bowl.

3. One at a time, dip the shrimp into the mustard mixture to coat all but the tails (use the tip of a finger to fill in any bare spots), then roll them into the pecans to coat them well.

4. Arrange the shrimp in a single layer on the baking sheet and bake, turning once, until browned on both sides, 10 to 12 minutes. Serve hot with Red Pepper-Horseradish Mayonnaise for dipping.

RED PEPPER—HORSERADISH MAYONNAISE

MAKES ABOUT 1½ CUPS

1 roasted red pepper, seeded, peeled, and coarsely chopped
1 cup mayonnaise
1 tablespoon prepared horseradish
A few drops hot pepper sauce

Combine the red pepper and mayonnaise in the bowl of a food processor fitted with the steel chopping blade and process until smooth. Add the horseradish and process to blend. Season to taste with hot pepper sauce. Transfer to a small bowl, cover, and chill until needed.

A pile of goose down pillows

Grilled Peanut Butter, Bacon, and Banana Sandwich

MAKES 1

Ever since I was knee-high to a grasshopper, this has been one of my favorite treats. It's a great midday or midnight snack and I've even been known to make myself one for a quick supper.

The quantities can be adjusted to your own taste, but here's the basic idea. (You can really only fit about half a banana's worth of slices onto the bread, but it won't be a problem—I'll bet you'll end up making two sandwiches, anyway.)

1 tablespoon softened butter
2 slices firm, good-quality white
    or whole grain bread
2 to 3 tablespoons chunky
    peanut butter
½ ripe banana, thinly sliced
3 slices crisply cooked bacon

1. Generously butter one side of each slice of bread, then turn the slices over, buttered side down. Spread each slice very generously with peanut butter. Cover 1 slice of bread with a single layer of banana slices and cover the other slice of bread with a layer of bacon. Carefully turn the bacon-topped slice over onto the banana-topped slice.

2. Place the sandwich in a small skillet over medium-low heat and cook until nicely browned on both sides. When done, cut the sandwich diagonally into quarters (somehow it tastes better cut like this) and eat right away.

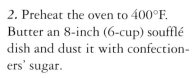

Southern Comfort Soufflé with Sliced Strawberries

SERVES 6 TO 8

An airy soufflé, though certainly not a "light" dessert, can be the perfect ending to a fancy dinner. Don't be scared off by the soufflé's temperamental reputation— this recipe's never failed me.

8 large egg yolks, lightly beaten
⅔ cup sugar
⅓ cup Southern Comfort liqueur
1 teaspoon grated orange rind
10 large egg whites
¼ teaspoon cream of tartar
1 pint strawberries, hulled and thinly sliced

1. In the top of a double boiler over simmering water, combine the egg yolks and sugar and cook, whisking constantly, until the mixture forms a wide ribbon when dropped from the whisk. Remove the pan from the heat, stir in the Southern Comfort and orange rind, and allow to cool.

2. Preheat the oven to 400°F. Butter an 8-inch (6-cup) soufflé dish and dust it with confectioners' sugar.

3. In a clean bowl, beat the egg whites until soft peaks form. Add the cream of tartar and continue beating until stiff peaks form.

4. A third at a time, carefully fold the cooled egg yolk mixture into the egg white mixture. Gently spoon the mixture into the prepared soufflé dish.

5. Bake until the soufflé is firm and nicely browned, about 15 minutes. Serve warm, spooned into individual serving dishes and topped with strawberries.

$\mathcal{S}$moked Salmon and Caviar Roulades with Whole Wheat Blini

MAKES ABOUT 3 DOZEN
HORS D'OEUVRES

One could say a little goes a long way, but in this case it never does. Just assume that no matter how much you have, it will never be enough. The roulade recipe comes from my caviar-loving friend Pam Thomas.

ROULADES

6 scallions, white and green
   parts, finely chopped
1 tablespoon chopped dill
2 large eggs, hard-boiled
   and mashed
1/2 cup sour cream
4 ounces cream cheese, softened
8 ounces thinly sliced smoked
   salmon
4 ounces (or 1 3 1/2-ounce jar)
   salmon caviar

BLINI

1/2 cup sifted whole wheat flour
1/2 cup sifted all-purpose flour
1/2 teaspoon baking powder
1/4 teaspoon salt
1 1/8 cups milk
3 tablespoons butter, melted
   and cooled
2 large eggs

1. Combine the scallions, dill, eggs, sour cream, and cream cheese. Cut the salmon slices in half crosswise, then cut into 1/2-

inch-wide strips. Spread a teaspoon of the sour cream mixture onto a slice of salmon and add a few grains of caviar. Roll up, jelly roll fashion. Chill until needed.

2. In a mixing bowl, sift together the flours, baking powder, and salt. Add the milk, butter, and eggs and beat until blended. Let the batter stand 20 minutes.

3. In a skillet over medium heat, heat a thin film of oil until sizzling (or use a nonstick electric skillet or griddle, heated to 350°F.). Drop the batter by tablespoonfuls into the skillet and cook until the surface is bubbly all over, about 2 minutes. Flip the blini with a spatula and brown on the other sides. Transfer to a plate and keep warm while cooking the remaining blini.

4. To serve, arrange the blini on a platter and top each one with a roulade. Garnish each with a few grains of caviar and a tiny sprig of dill.

*A tropical vacation
in the dead of winter*

The Ultimate Carrot Cake, with Pineapple-Coconut Frosting

MAKES ONE 9-INCH ROUND, 2-LAYER CAKE

When carrot cakes burst onto the scene some years ago, their popularity soared as we all jumped to eat this "healthy" dessert. Well, you know and I know that a carrot cake is no better or worse for us than any chocolate dessert as far as calories are concerned. So, let's just accept reality and go at it.

¾ cup firmly packed light brown sugar
1 cup granulated sugar
4 large eggs, lightly beaten
2 teaspoons vanilla extract
1 cup vegetable oil
2 cups all-purpose flour
2 teaspoons baking soda
½ teaspoon salt
2 teaspoons ground cinnamon
1 teaspoon ground ginger
¼ teaspoon grated nutmeg
2 cups (about ¾ pound) grated carrots
1 8½-ounce can crushed pineapple in juice, drained
1 cup shredded coconut
1 cup chopped walnuts, toasted

FROSTING

*1 8-ounce package cream
  cheese, softened*
3/8 cup (3/4 stick) butter, softened
1 teaspoon vanilla extract
3 cups confectioners' sugar
*1 8 1/2-ounce can crushed
  pineapple in juice, drained*
*1 cup shredded coconut, lightly
  toasted*

1. Preheat the oven to 350°F. Grease two 9-inch cake pans, line them with wax paper, then grease the wax paper.

2. In a mixing bowl, combine the sugars, eggs, and vanilla and beat until smooth. Gradually beat in the oil. In a separate bowl, sift together the flour, baking soda, salt, and spices. Beat the dry mixture into the wet mixture, beating until smooth, then stir in the carrots, pineapple, coconut, and nuts.

3. Divide the batter between the prepared pans and bake until the edges begin to pull away from the pan and a cake tester or toothpick inserted in the center comes out clean, 35 to 40 minutes. Turn the layers out onto wire racks to cool completely, then gently pull off the wax paper.

4. To make the frosting, combine the cream cheese, butter, and vanilla in a medium bowl and beat until smooth. Gradually beat in the confectioners' sugar, then stir in the pineapple. Frost the tops and sides of the cake, then cover the frosting with the toasted coconut.

*A long, steamy
bubble bath*

A few bottles of that fabulously good wine

Rigatoni with Wild Mushrooms

SERVES 4

One of my favorite memories from a trip through eastern Europe a few years ago is of being served the local wild mushrooms that are foraged at night. Back home, all kinds of wonderful wild mushrooms are now showing up in grocery stores, and discovering new ones is always a treat.

Mushrooms have such an exquisite woodsy flavor, yet we often muck them up with a lot of other stuff. This simple recipe lets the wild mushrooms shine, and that's my idea of heaven.

16 ounces assorted wild mushrooms (shiitake, Portobello, porcini, morels, etc.)
2 garlic cloves, crushed
2 tablespoons extra-virgin olive oil
2 tablespoons butter
½ cup rich chicken stock (see Note)
½ cup heavy cream
¾ cup chopped spinach leaves
Salt and freshly ground black pepper
1 pound rigatoni
¼ cup grated Romano cheese

1. Cut the mushrooms into ⅛-inch-thick slices. Slices of larger mushrooms may have to be cut in half and tiny mushrooms can be left whole. Pierce the garlic cloves with toothpicks (this will make them easy to remove later).

2. Combine the oil, butter, and garlic in a skillet over medium heat and heat until the fat is sizzling. Add the mushrooms and sauté until they are tender and turning golden, 5 to 7 minutes.

3. Add the stock and cream and turn the heat to medium-high. Bring to a simmer and cook, stirring constantly, until the sauce thickens slightly, about 5 minutes longer. Remove and discard the garlic cloves. Add the spinach and simmer 3 more minutes. Season to taste with salt and plenty of pepper.

4. Meanwhile, place a kettle of salted water over high heat and bring to a boil. Add the pasta and cook until al dente (the timing will vary; check the package for directions). When the pasta is done, drain it and

divide it among 4 serving plates or shallow bowls.

5. Spoon the mushrooms and sauce over the pasta. Sprinkle 1 tablespoon cheese over each serving and add a grind of black pepper. Serve immediately and pass more grated cheese.

NOTE: Low-sodium canned stock can be used; reduce $\frac{2}{3}$ cup stock to $\frac{1}{2}$ cup.

Scalloped Oysters

SERVES 6 TO 8

I *hated* oysters when I was a kid (Dad loved them, so Mom fixed them more often than I would have liked). I really can't remember when that changed, but now I never meet an oyster I don't like.

This rich dish is traditional down South during the holiday season, especially as part of a big Christmas or Christmas Eve dinner. I like making it as the center of a simple supper, with just a green salad on the side.

½ cup (1 stick) butter
1 medium onion, finely chopped
½ stalk celery, with leaves, finely chopped
2 cups fine, dry bread crumbs or cracker crumbs
½ cup chopped parsley
2 pints shucked oysters, with their liquor
1 cup (½ pint) heavy cream
2 teaspoons Worcestershire sauce
½ teaspoon salt
½ teaspoon hot pepper sauce
Paprika

1. Preheat the oven to 400°F. Lightly oil a shallow 1½-quart baking dish.

2. In a medium skillet, melt the butter. Add the onion and celery to the skillet and sauté until golden, 5 to 7 minutes. Add the crumbs and sauté until they begin to brown (the mixture will be rather dry). Stir in the parsley, then transfer the crumb mixture to a bowl and reserve.

3. Drain the oyster liquor into the skillet, reserving the oysters. Add the cream, Worcestershire sauce, salt, and hot pepper sauce and mix well. Bring to a simmer and cook, stirring frequently, until the mixture is slightly thickened, 5 to 7 minutes.

4. Place about ⅓ of the oysters in a single layer in the baking dish, cover evenly with about ⅓ of the crumb mixture, then spoon about ⅓ of the cream mixture over all. Repeat twice. Sprinkle the top generously with paprika.

5. Bake until the dish is bubbly all over and the top is nicely browned, 25 to 30 minutes. (If the top begins to get too brown, cover the pan loosely with foil.) Serve immediately.

TWO DOZEN
OYSTERS ON THE
HALF SHELL

Forget about making "cocktail sauce" ahead of time—serve freshly shucked oysters the way they do in the real oyster bars, from Maine to New Orleans: Pour some ketchup into small fluted paper cups, then pass the bottles of Worcestershire, Tabasco, and horseradish, along with lots of lemon wedges. Everyone mixes his own and dives right in.

Banana Split Foster

SERVES 2

A combination of the best two gooey banana desserts I know, this is actually a little closer to the New Orleans classic, Bananas Foster. But serving it up in a banana split dish makes it all the more extravagant, especially with the over-the-top topping of crunchy Crushed Praline (though plain toasted chopped pecans will do in a pinch), a mound of whipped cream, and a cherry.

¼ *cup (½ stick) butter*
¼ *cup firmly packed dark*
   brown sugar

½ *teaspoon ground cinnamon*
2 *ripe bananas*
¼ *cup dark rum*
6 *small scoops (about 1 pint)*
   best-quality vanilla ice cream
½ *cup heavy cream, whipped*
Crushed Praline (recipe
   follows)
Toasted pecan halves
2 *fresh or maraschino cherries,*
   with stems

1. In a small, heavy skillet over medium-low heat, melt the butter, then add the brown sugar and cinnamon, stirring until the brown sugar is melted and blended in.

2. Cut the bananas in half lengthwise, then add the bananas

to the skillet and sauté until heated through, 3 to 4 minutes. Stir the rum into the pan and allow the mixture to heat through. Remove the pan from the heat and, using a long match, ignite. Carefully baste the bananas with the flaming sauce.

3. When the flames die out, arrange 2 banana halves each along the sides of 2 banana split dishes. Working quickly, place 3 scoops of ice cream in each dish, then spoon the sauce over the ice cream. Top with whipped cream, a sprinkling of Crushed Praline, pecan halves, and a cherry.

CRUSHED PRALINE
½ cup sugar
2 tablespoons water
½ cup chopped pecans

Combine the sugar and water in a small, heavy saucepan over low heat and stir until the sugar is dissolved. Raise the heat and boil rapidly without stirring until the syrup turns a light golden brown, 5 to 7 minutes. Stir in the pecans and pour the mixture out onto a lightly greased baking sheet, then allow to cool. Chop the mixture fine in the bowl of a food processor fitted with the steel chopping blade.

Taking a cruise to nowhere

Old-Fashioned Devil's Food Cake with Mocha Buttercream Frosting

MAKES ONE 9-INCH ROUND, 2-LAYER CAKE

Devil's food cake is my brother Joe's favorite, but we never seemed to have it except once a year, on his birthday. I suppose it became kind of a tradition—it just wouldn't have been special if we had it all the time.

Unsweetened cocoa, for dusting
²/₃ cup (1¹/₃ sticks) unsalted butter, softened
1³/₄ cups sugar
3 large eggs
1¹/₂ teaspoons vanilla extract
2 cups all-purpose flour
²/₃ cup unsweetened cocoa
¹/₄ teaspoon baking powder
1¹/₄ teaspoons baking soda
1 teaspoon salt
¹/₂ cup buttermilk or plain yogurt
¹/₂ cup cold strong coffee
(it's okay to use instant)

FROSTING

1 cup (2 sticks) unsalted butter, softened
1½ cups confectioners' sugar
6 ounces (6 squares) semisweet chocolate, melted and cooled
1 teaspoon instant espresso powder
1 teaspoon vanilla extract

1. Preheat the oven to 350°F. Grease two 9-inch round cake pans and dust them lightly with cocoa.

2. In a mixing bowl, cream the butter and sugar until light and fluffy, then beat in the eggs and vanilla. In a separate bowl, sift together the flour, cocoa, baking powder, baking soda, and salt. In a measuring cup, combine the buttermilk and coffee. Beat this mixture alternately with the dry ingredients into the butter mixture, beating well after each addition until smooth.

3. Divide the batter between the prepared pans. Bake until a cake tester or toothpick inserted in the center comes out clean, about 30 minutes. Turn the layers out onto wire racks and cool completely before frosting.

4. To make the frosting, cream the butter and confectioners' sugar together until light and fluffy, 2 to 3 minutes. Add the chocolate, espresso powder, and vanilla and beat until the frosting is creamy and smooth, 2 to 3 minutes longer. Use the frosting when the cake has cooled.

A cashmere muffler

Lamb, Pork, and Sausage Cassoulet

SERVES 8

On a cold night, there's nothing more comforting than having a cassoulet bubbling away in the oven, its aromas of garlic and herbs enveloping the whole house. And for me, the anticipation has almost as much impact as the eating itself. Serve the cassoulet with a bottle of good red wine and a green salad, with fruit and cheese for dessert.

1 pound Great Northern beans
1/2 pound slab bacon, cut into
    1/4-inch dice
4 1-inch-thick loin lamb chops
4 1-inch-thick loin pork chops
1 pound garlic sausage or
    kielbasa, diagonally cut into
    1/2-inch-thick slices
1 pound sweet Italian sausage,
    cut into 1-inch pieces
3 medium onions, chopped
6 large garlic cloves, chopped
1/2 cup dry white
    wine

3 cups (1 28-ounce can) canned
    crushed Italian plum tomatoes
1 1/2 teaspoons dried thyme
1 1/2 teaspoons dried basil
1/2 cup chopped parsley
3 bay leaves
Freshly ground black pepper
1/2 cup fine fresh bread crumbs
3 tablespoons butter, melted

1. Pick over the beans and rinse well. Place in a large saucepan with water to cover. Place the pan on the stove and bring to a boil. Turn off the heat, cover the pan, and allow the beans to soak 1 hour.

2. Place the bacon in a 4-quart Dutch oven and sauté until the fat is well rendered, about 10 minutes. Remove the meat with a slotted spoon and reserve. Then remove all but 2 tablespoons fat from the Dutch oven and reserve.

3. While the bacon is sautéing, cut the meat from the chops into 3/4-inch chunks and reserve the bones. After removing the bacon from the pan, add the other meat and sauté until browned on all

sides, about 10 minutes. Remove the meat and reserve. Sauté the sausage until brown on all sides, then remove it and reserve.

4. Add enough reserved fat to the Dutch oven to make about 3 tablespoons. Add the onions and garlic and sauté until golden, 5 to 7 minutes. Add the wine, raise the heat, and simmer for 2 or 3 minutes, scraping up anybrowned bits from the bottom of the pan.

5. Add the tomatoes, herbs, and reserved bones to the pan.Bring to a simmer, lower the heat, cover, and simmer, stirring occasionally to prevent sticking, for 30 minutes. The sauce should be fairly thick. Remove the bones and discard them. Season the sauce to taste with plenty of pepper (do not salt —the bacon will add plenty of saltiness to the finished cassoulet).

6. Preheat the oven to 325°F.

7. Return all the reserved meats to the Dutch oven. Drain the beans, reserving about 1 cup liquid, then add the beans to the

Dutch oven. Carefully stir to mix all the ingredients. Sprinkle the bread crumbs over the surface, then drizzle the melted butter over the crumbs.

8. Place the Dutch oven in the oven and bake, uncovered, for 2 hours, or until the beans are tender and the top is well browned. Check periodically during baking and, if the cassoulet seems a little dry, add a bit of the reserved bean liquid. Serve hot.

Peach Melba Shortcakes

MAKES 4

By luck of nature, peaches and raspberries are available at the same time, and when they're combined, it's always a good marriage. Add whipped cream, and it's heaven.

RASPBERRY PUREE
½ pint raspberries
½ cup sugar

SHORTCAKES
⅞ cup sifted all-purpose flour
2 teaspoons sugar
¼ teaspoon salt

1½ teaspoons baking powder
½ teaspoon ground cinnamon
½ teaspoon ground ginger
2 tablespoons cold butter
⅓ cup milk

2 cups sliced ripe peaches
1 cup (½ pint) heavy cream, whipped to soft peaks
¼ cup lightly toasted sliced almonds

1. To make the puree, combine the berries and sugar in a small, heavy saucepan over medium heat and cook, stirring constantly, until the raspberries begin to break up and the sugar is dissolved, 5 to 7 minutes. Remove from the heat and press the mixture through a sieve into a small bowl to puree the berries and remove the seeds. Cover and chill at least 2 hours before using.

2. Preheat the oven to 425°F. Lightly grease a baking sheet.

3. In a large mixing bowl, combine the flour, sugar, salt, baking powder, and spices, then cut in the butter with a pastry blender or 2 knives. Stir in the milk and mix until the dry ingredients are just moistened, forming a somewhat sticky dough.

4. Transfer the dough to a floured work surface and pat it out to a thickness of about ⅜ inch. Using a 3-inch round biscuit cutter or a cookie cutter, cut out shortcakes and place them on the baking sheet. Bake the shortcakes until they are well risen and lightly browned, about 15 minutes. Remove to a wire rack to cool.

5. To serve, split the shortcakes in half and place the bottom halves in individual serving dishes. Spoon the peaches over the shortcake bottoms, reserving 4 perfect slices. Use about ¾ of the whipped cream to top the peaches, then add the shortcake tops. Spoon the raspberry puree over the shortcakes, then top each with a dab of whipped cream, a sprinkling of sliced almonds, and a peach slice.

A ride up, up, and away in a hot air balloon

Champagne Sorbet with Cranberry-Almond Wafers

MAKES ABOUT 1½ PINTS

Anything made with Champagne is special and this cool and refreshing sorbet is the most wonderful way I know to end a rich meal. The cranberry wafers make it a complete, "well-rounded" dessert.

1 cup water
1 cup sugar
2 tablespoons light corn syrup
Juice and grated rind
of ½ lemon

1½ cups dry Champagne
2 large egg whites
2 tablespoons confectioners' sugar
Cranberry-Almond Wafers
(recipe follows)

1. In a small, heavy saucepan, combine the water and sugar and place over medium-high heat. Cook, stirring constantly, until the sugar is dissolved. Stir in the corn syrup and the lemon juice and rind, remove from the heat, and cool.

2. Stir in the Champagne, pour into a freezer tray or other shallow dish, and cover tightly with plastic wrap. Place the pan in the freezer and freeze until the mixture is almost frozen through, 2 to 3 hours, stirring every half hour or so to ensure even freezing.

3. In a small bowl, beat the egg whites until soft peaks form, then gradually beat in the confectioners' sugar, beating until stiff but not dry. Transfer the freezer mixture to the bowl of a food processor fitted with the

CRANBERRY—ALMOND WAFERS

MAKES ABOUT 3 DOZEN

½ cup (1 stick) butter, softened
½ cup sugar
1 large egg
½ teaspoon vanilla extract
½ teaspoon almond extract
⅞ cup sifted all-purpose flour
½ cup finely chopped almonds
½ cup finely chopped cranberries

1. Preheat the oven to 350°F. Lightly grease baking sheets.

2. In a mixing bowl, cream the butter and sugar until light and fluffy, then beat in the egg, vanilla, and almond extract. Gradually add the flour, beating constantly until smooth. Stir in the almonds and cranberries.

3. Drop the dough by teaspoonfuls about 2 inches apart onto the baking sheets. Bake until the edges of the cookies are lightly browned, about 10 minutes. Remove the cookies to wire racks to cool, then store in tightly covered containers in a cool place.

steel chopping blade and process just until smooth. Fold in the egg white mixture.

4. Place the mixture in the freezer pan and freeze until slushy. Stir the mixture and freeze until firm. About 15 minutes before serving, transfer the pan to the refrigerator to allow the sorbet to soften slightly. Just before serving, spoon the sorbet into footed glasses and add 2 Cranberry-Almond Wafers to each glass.

When I took my first trip to London, I was traveling with a friend who jabbered constantly beforehand about the English custom of having tea in the afternoon. Not being much of a tea drinker, I thought, "How silly" and "Why would I want to interrupt seeing all the sights to do such a thing?" Well, at four o'clock on our first afternoon, I found myself seated in a high-backed chair in a comfortable room off the lobby at Claridge's Hotel. The room looked like my grandmother's parlor (on a slightly grander scale!) but with the addition of gleaming trolleys laden with little sandwiches, tiny desserts, and scones accompanied by silver bowls of strawberry jam and clotted cream. What an extraordinary way to spend the end of an afternoon!

*C*urrant *Tea Scones with Clotted Cream and Wild Strawberry Jam*

MAKES 1 DOZEN

Scones themselves aren't particularly sinful—what's eaten with them is. Alas, the traditional clotted cream served with scones in England is not very available here, but I've provided an equally rich, easy substitute. And use a good brand of English wild strawberry jam.

2 cups all-purpose flour
2 tablespoons sugar
¼ teaspoon salt
2½ teaspoons baking powder
¼ cup (½ stick) cold butter
½ cup dried currants
2 large eggs
½ cup heavy cream
Mock Clotted Cream (recipe
  follows)
Wild strawberry jam

1. Preheat the oven to 400°F. Lightly grease a baking sheet.

2. In a mixing bowl, sift together the flour, sugar, salt, and baking powder. Using a pastry blender or 2 knives, cut in the butter. Stir in the currants.

3. In a separate small bowl, combine the eggs and cream and beat with a fork until well blended. Reserving 2 tablespoons of this mixture, pour it over the dry mixture and stir with the fork until the dry ingredients are just moistened.

4. Transfer the dough to a floured work surface and, using floured hands, pat it out to a thickness of about ½ inch. Using a floured knife, cut the dough into approximate 3-inch squares, then cut the squares diagonally in half

5. Carefully place the scones on the prepared baking sheet and brush the reserved egg mixture over the surface. Bake until the scones have risen and are golden brown, about 10 minutes. Serve immediately, or transfer to a wire rack to cool and serve at room temperature. Split the scones and pass the Mock Clotted Cream and wild strawberry jam.

MOCK CLOTTED CREAM
1 cup (½ pint) heavy cream
1 cup sour cream
2 tablespoons confectioners' sugar
Pinch of salt

Combine the two creams in a small bowl or jar, cover tightly, and let stand at room temperature for 12 hours or overnight, until the mixture thickens. Stir in the sugar and salt and chill for 24 hours. Store in the refrigerator up to a week. Just before serving, the cream can be whipped a bit to make it fluffy.

Champagne
Cocktails

MAGNOLIAS

MAKES 8 SERVINGS

Champagne adds a boost to any occasion, and sipping these Champagne and juice cocktails out on the porch can help make even a muggy summer evening a pleasant one.

1 bottle chilled Champagne
2 cups chilled grapefruit juice
1/4 cup any red berry liqueur,
such as Chambord (raspberry)
or Boggs (cranberry)
Mint sprigs, for garnish

Combine the Champagne, juice, and liqueur in a glass pitcher and stir to blend. Serve immediately in Champagne flutes or wineglasses, garnished with the mint.

FRESH RASPBERRY KIR

The classic kir—Champagne in a flute with a splash of crème de cassis—first became popular with Café Society during the thirties. I like this new version just a little bit better.

Raspberries
Raspberry Puree (page 46)
Chilled Champagne

For each cocktail, place 3 or 4 raspberries in the bottom of a Champagne flute, then add 2 tablespoons Raspberry Puree. Fill each flute about ⅔ full with Champagne (do not stir!) and serve immediately. Cheers!

Simple Chocolate Truffles

MAKES ABOUT 2 DOZEN

These little sweets, offering just a bite, are a nice surprise for anyone who's a chocaholic.

4 ounces (4 squares) semisweet chocolate, melted and cooled
1 3-ounce package cream cheese, softened
1²⁄₃ cups confectioners' sugar, sifted
¼ teaspoon vanilla extract
¼ teaspoon rum (or peppermint, almond, or coconut) extract

COATINGS
Toasted coconut, finely crumbled
Chocolate jimmies
Confectioners' sugar
Finely chopped toasted nuts (hazelnuts, almonds, or pecans)
Finely crushed peppermint stick candy
Crushed Praline (page 41)
¼ cup unsweetened cocoa mixed with 2 teaspoons confectioners' sugar and ½ teaspoon ground cinnamon

1. In a mixing bowl, combine the chocolate, cream cheese, sugar, and extracts and beat until blended and smooth. Roll this "dough" into ¾-inch balls, then roll the balls in one or several of the coatings.

2. Place in single layers in a wax paper–lined container and chill thoroughly until firm.

$\mathcal{B}$lueberry Cheese Tart

MAKES ONE 9-INCH TART

A rich cheesecake filling in an orange pastry crust is topped with a layer of glazed berries. Mmmm.

ORANGE PASTRY CRUST
1½ cups all-purpose flour
Scant ½ teaspoon salt
1½ teaspooons sugar
¼ cup vegetable shortening, chilled
¼ cup (½ stick) cold butter
Grated rind of 1 small orange
3 to 4 tablespoons orange juice

FILLING
1 8-ounce package cream cheese, softened
6 tablespoons (¾ stick) unsalted butter, softened
⅓ cup sugar
2 large eggs
1 teaspoon vanilla extract
⅔ cup seedless raspberry fruit spread
1 pint blueberries
1 thin orange slice, cut into wedges, for garnish

1. To make the crust, first sift the flour, salt, and sugar together in a mixing bowl. Using your fingertips, rub the fats into the dry ingredients until coarse and crumbly in texture. Do this quickly to keep the fats cold and solid. (Or use a pastry blender to combine the dry ingredients and the shortenings.) Stir in the orange rind.

2. Starting with 3 tablespoon-fuls, add the orange juice and work into the flour-shortening mixture to form a ball of dough.

Add 1 or more teaspoons of juice if necessary to hold the dough together. Wrap the dough ball in wax paper and chill for 1 hour.

3. Preheat the oven to 350°F. Roll out the pastry and use it to line a 9-inch tart pan with a removable bottom. Prick the pastry all over with a fork and bake for 10 minutes, then remove the pan from the oven.

4. In a mixing bowl, combine the cream cheese, butter, and sugar and beat until smooth, then beat in the eggs. Add the vanilla and mix well.

5. Place the fruit spread in a small, heavy saucepan over low heat and stir until melted, then brush about ¼ of the spread over the pastry, reserving the remainder. Transfer the cream cheese mixture to the pie shell.

6. Bake until the crust is nicely browned and the filling is set, about 25 minutes (The filling will puff up during baking but it will settle again as it cools.) Remove the pan to a wire rack and allow the tart to cool.

7. Arrange the blueberries in an even layer over the cheese filling. Reheat the remaining fruit spread and drizzle it over the berries, glazing them completely. Chill the tart for 2 hours before serving.

Taking the afternoon off simply because it's a beautiful day

Café au Lait

MAKES 4 SERVINGS

In New Orleans, café au lait is brewed with the local extra-strong blend of coffee that includes chicory. The Louisiana blend isn't easy to find, so, as an alternative, I use a good French roast, adding $1\frac{1}{2}$ times the amount of freshly ground beans to the pot.

2 cups freshly brewed extra-strength coffee
$1\frac{1}{2}$ cups scalded milk
Sugar to taste

Pour enough piping hot coffee into a big heavy mug (no delicate teacups, please) to fill it a little more than halfway, then fill the mug with the hot milk. Spoon in a little or a lot of sugar, stir, and wake up.

BREAKFAST IN BED

It's raining outside, it's cozy inside—a nice morning to stay in bed. But after a while, hunger pangs strike, and no one's around to make you breakfast. So downstairs you go. As you're fixing a warm and comforting breakfast, the wind picks up and the rain gets heavier....Well, there's no one around, remember? So once breakfast is ready, you take it upstairs and crawl right back under the covers. Oh, if only this were true!

Powdered Sugar Beignets

MAKES 12 TO 16

There are a few must-dos when anyone goes to New Orleans, and one of them is having beignets and café au lait in the morning at Café du Monde. I like to get up really early to beat the crowds, then walk up the levee with my breakfast to watch the busy river go by. Ahhhh. Here's an extra-rich, sugar-covered version so you can have beignets any time.

> *Vegetable oil or shortening, for frying*
> *½ cup (1 stick) unsalted butter*
> *1 cup hot tap water*
> *1 cup sifted all-purpose flour*
> *2 tablespoons sugar*
> *¼ teaspoon salt*
> *Pinch of nutmeg*
> *4 large eggs, at room temperature*
> *Confectioners' sugar, for dusting*

1. Place enough oil or shortening in a deep fryer (or a large, heavy saucepan fitted with a frying or candy thermometer) to fill it about halfway. Slowly bring the shortening to a temperature of 365°F.

2. In a heavy saucepan, combine the butter and water, place over medium heat, and bring to a boil. In a small bowl, stir the flour, sugar, salt, and nutmeg together, then, using a whisk or hand mixer, beat the dry ingredients into the ingredients in the pan. Continue beating until the mixture forms a ball, about 1 minute.

3. Remove the pan from the heat and beat in the eggs one at a time, beating well after each addition.

4. Drop the dough by heaping teaspoonfuls into the hot fat, using a second spoon to help shape and scoop off the dough. Fry until the beignets are puffed and a rich golden brown and remove to absorbent paper to drain. Dust the beignets very generously with confectioners' sugar (half the fun of eating them is getting sugar all over yourself) and serve warm.

$\mathcal{A}$ Mess of Hush Puppies

MAKES ABOUT 3 DOZEN

Hush puppies are traditionally served with fried fish but I can make a meal of them all by themselves. Crunchy on the outside and tender on the inside, subtly oniony and slightly spicy, these are the stuff that dreams are made of.

2¼ cups stone-ground yellow
*   cornmeal*
2 teaspoons baking powder
1 teaspoon salt
2 teaspoons sugar
1 small onion, finely chopped
1 cup milk
2 large eggs, lightly beaten

½ teaspoon hot pepper sauce,
*   or more to taste*
Vegetable oil or shortening, for
*   frying*

1. In a mixing bowl, combine the cornmeal, baking powder, salt, and sugar. Stir until well blended, then stir in the onion. Add the milk, egg, and hot pepper sauce and stir until the dry ingredients are just moistened, making a sticky dough.

2. Place enough oil or shortening in a large, heavy saucepan or a deep fryer to reach a depth of about 4 inches. Place over medium heat and bring to the point of almost smoking (about 370°F. on a frying or candy thermometer).

3. Using floured hands, form the dough into 1-inch balls. Drop no more than 6 or 7 dough balls at a time into the hot fat and fry until a rich golden brown, 4 to 5 minutes. Using a slotted spoon, remove the hush puppies to absorbent paper to drain while frying the rest. Serve warm.

$\mathcal{R}$ipe tomatoes in winter

$\mathcal{R}$aspberry Fool

SERVES 4

1 cup ($^1/_2$ pint) heavy cream
$^1/_2$ teaspoon salt
$^1/_2$ teaspoon vanilla extract
1 recipe Raspberry Puree
   (page 46)
Whole raspberries, for garnish

No more than 2 hours before
serving, combine the cream, salt,
and vanilla in a medium bowl
and whip until soft peaks form.
Fold in the berry pureé, then
spoon the fool into stemmed
glasses. Chill. Garnish with
whole raspberries just before
serving.

An orchid plant

Brownie Pudding-Cake "All the Way"

SERVES 8 TO 10

My favorite chocolate dessert of all is a brownie and my favorite way of having a brownie is "all the way," topped with ice cream and hot fudge. This pudding-cake, an old-fashioned Midwestern dessert that's still popular back home, fits the bill perfectly: as the cake bakes it separates, making a warm, fudgy sauce on the bottom. I like it best two ways—with mint-chocolate chip ice cream or with vanilla ice cream and berries—but you may have other ideas.

⅜ *cup (¾ stick) unsalted butter,*
  softened
1¾ *cups sugar*
2 *large eggs*
½ *cup milk*
1½ *teaspoons vanilla extract*
1 *cup all-purpose flour*
½ *teaspoon salt*
1 *teaspoon baking powder*
⅔ *cup unsweetened cocoa*
¾ *cup chopped nuts*
1 *pint ice cream*

1. Preheat the oven to 350°F. Lightly grease an 8-inch sqaure cake pan.

2. In a mixing bowl, cream together the butter and 1 cup of the sugar, then beat in the eggs, milk, and vanilla. In a separate bowl, sift together the flour, salt, baking powder, and ⅓ cup of the cocoa. Add the dry mixture to the wet mixture and stir until the dry ingredients are just blended in. Stir the nuts into the batter.

3. Spread the batter evenly into the prepared pan. In a small, heavy saucepan, combine the remaining ¾ cup sugar, the remaining ⅓ cup cocoa, and 1¼ cups hot tap water. Place over medium-high heat and bring to a simmer, stirring until the sugar is dissolved and the mixture is fairly smooth.

4. Pour the saucepan mixture over the batter in the pan and place the pan in the oven. Bake until a toothpick or cake tester inserted halfway into the center

of the cake comes out clean, about 35 minutes. Remove the pan to a wire rack and cool about 15 minutes before serving.

5. To serve, cut the warm cake into squares. Place the squares into individual serving dishes, then top with scoops of ice cream. Spoon some of the sauce from the pan over each serving and dig right in.

Garlic-Laced Mashed Potatoes

SERVES 4 AS A SIDE DISH

Is there anyone who doesn't love mashed potatoes? Garlic? Butter? Well, here they are, all at once.

6 tablespoons (¾ stick) butter
1 large head garlic, separated into cloves and peeled
1 ½ pounds Idaho potatoes, peeled and cut into eighths
1 cup milk
Salt and white pepper to taste

1. Melt half of the butter in a small saucepan over low heat, then add the garlic cloves. Cover the pan and cook the garlic, stirring occasionally, until golden and very tender, about 20 minutes. Transfer the mixture to a food processor and puree.

2. Meanwhile, place the potatoes in a large saucepan with salted water to cover. Place the pan over medium-high heat and boil the potatoes until tender, about 20 minutes.

3. Drain the potatoes and mash with a potato masher. Add the remaining butter and the milk and beat with a wooden spoon until light and fluffy (add a bit more milk if needed). Beat in the garlic puree, season with salt and pepper, and serve.

Chocolate-Dipped Strawberries with Pistachios

MAKES 20 TO 24

No matter where these turn up, they always bring a smile. They're one of those simple little confections that go a long way toward making anyone feel good.

4 ounces (4 squares) semisweet chocolate, coarsely chopped
1 tablespoon brandy
½ cup finely chopped roasted pistachios
20 to 24 jumbo strawberries, preferably with stems

1. In a small, heavy saucepan over low heat, combine the chocolate and brandy. Stir until the chocolate is melted and the mixture is smooth.

2. Place the pistachios in a shallow bowl. One at a time, dip a berry halfway into the chocolate mixture, then quickly dip one side into the nuts, covering about half the chocolate. Place the berries on wax paper to cool, then store in tightly covered containers in a cool place, for up to 24 hours before serving.

*G*iving a loved one
"just what they've
always wanted..."

RECITE INDEX

Banana Split Foster, 40
Belgian Fries, 14
Blueberry Cheese Tart, 54
Brownie Pudding-Cake "All
the Way," 60
Café au Lait, 56
Champagne Cocktails, 52
Champagne Sorbet with
Cranberry-Almond Wafers, 48
Cherries Jubilee, 21
Chicken-Fried Steaks with Cream
Gravy, 24
Chocolate-Dipped Strawberries
with Pistachios, 63
Chocolate-Filled Almond Cream
Puffs, 16
Currant Tea Scones with
Clotted Cream and Wild
Strawberry Jam, 50
Garlic-Laced Mashed Potatoes, 62
Grilled Peanut Butter, Bacon,
and Banana Sandwich, 30
Hazelnut-Fudge Bread Puddings,
6
Jumbo Chocolate Chip Cookies, 20
Lamb, Pork, and Sausage
Cassoulet, 44
Lemon Charlotte with Raspberries,
10

Lobster Medallions in Port and
Peppercorn Sauce over Spinach
Fettuccine, 8
Maple-Walnut Sticky Buns, 26
Mess of Hush Puppies, A, 58
Mile-High Lime Chiffon Pie, 22
Old-Fashioned Devil's Food Cake
with Mocha Buttercream
Frosting, 42
Peach Melba Shortcakes, 46
Pecan-Deviled Shrimp with Red-
Pepper Horseradish
Mayonnaise, 28
Peppery Country Ham Pâté, 18
Powdered Sugar Beignets, 57
Raspberry Fool, 59
Rigatoni with Wild Mushrooms,
36
Salmon Steaks Puttanesca, 12
Scalloped Oysters, 38
Simple Chocolate Truffles, 53
Smoked Salmon and Caviar
Roulades with Whole Wheat
Blini, 32
Southern Comfort Soufflé with
Sliced Strawberries, 31
Ultimate Carrot Cake, with
Pineapple-Coconut Frosting,
The, 34